In The Kingdom
Of The Crow

Daniel Raven

ISBN: 1974503827
ISBN-13: 978-1974503827

When a man hides his past,
He has no future.

-Apache Proverb

I've found peace in madness…

Daniel Raven

INTRODUCTION

This book tries to characterize the meaning and purpose of life and death through prose,
 And fails miserably.

There is no true interpretation of life other than our own experience. Be it good or bad our eyes and ears, our lips and tongues, our nose and fingers all encompass our experience and define our story.
 And our life is just that, a story.
Enjoy it.
Feed it.
Be thankful for it.
Hate it.
Its all up to you.

Respectfully,

Daniel Raven

Daniel Raven

In the beginning the world was black and rough.
The sky cried in the darkness and smelled of fresh cut flowers.
One by one the animals left the forest.
Then,
      the wolf abandoned the land, and the young went to forage alone.

When the stars aligned and Ciowa could be seen from all directions the crow came, and with him he carried sacks of grain and sugar water. The pups ate and ate under the pale moon until one by one they burst.
There, the crow lay in wait.
Until his buried feathers brought on the sunrise.

In The Kingdom of The Crow

The past is a shadow.
The present, a guide.
The future,
        a dream.

Lost

Invited by the deserts dim sleep I went in search of you,
   And although my limbs were parched, my hope out weighed my sickness of despair. Such fear is most certainly the origin of my ill. Honored by this time long past and reflected in unison beyond the breathless rocks and blazing sun. the scorched earth seemed to center my souls pains to my two appendages below until I could take no more of either or all and surrendered myself to the sand.
   My last thoughts as always, were of you.
   Not a memory,
    not a dream in haste, just you.
   Your face.
   Your lips.
   Your smile.
   A wish finally realized in a moment of solace. Till the cruel beach enveloped me whole, and all but erased the memory of me.

Vanquished by my delusions
I hold repentance upon this vessels ruin
Awaiting the frost.

Beyond the heaving sea.
Where the sun sleeps
 and shadows hide.
I feel your presence,
 Your touch upon the wind.

Faith exists in absence.
Dwells within.
Sometimes weak,
 sometimes un yielding.
Always harbored by imagination.

Many years ago,

There was an un resting flame. Little wolf was said to have visited it in the time of the harvest, when the moon was at its fullest, and the grass smelled of mint and sage.

It was said he had a sickness of the mind. Always afraid, never giving to the great mother. Little wolf sought out the flame for help. Far from his people and the seasoned grass. Along his journey the earth became dry and froze under his feet, and the forest fell in famine, fire, and blood.

Still, little wolf pressed on. Mindful of every step. Careful and cautious not to anger the trees. Always afraid, always in doubt of his future.

Little wolf finally found the flame burning bright, high atop a mountain near the northern border. He looked deep within the center of its light. He held its gaze for hours, till his eyes could take no more, until its heat had taken his sight, and with it,

His fear of things to come.

Ain't my time yet is all.
Even if it was I ain't exceptin defeat.
Ill wrestle against the massacre of thoughtlessness,
 Till it chokes my every capillary.
Till I go all violently peaceful.
Even then,
 This here bag a bones is a house of memory,
 That'll share its secrets with the frost.

Sometimes I walk barefoot.
To remind my spirit of its ancestors.
To honor them,
 As they once were.
Proud and plentiful.
Giving and fierce.
Reminiscent of my vision quest with the great mother.
The day she made me one with the earth.

Here I lay interrupted
Scorning my past
 With a forked tongue.
Borrowing a languid smile
 From the drawer of doubt.
Raging within,
Grinning without.
Like a plump pig on Easter
Awaiting the kill.

My people exist simultaneously.
We are one nestled in the great mother den.
Words weaken the faith of man.
They make holes in the sky,
 Asking for angels and treasure.
Mother earth provides,
 And when we extinguish.
We feed the generation to come.

I am but a warrior caked in dirt awaiting absolution of sin.

Head just opened.
Like an egg.
Bits a meat creepin,
 Wasn't my fault.
Knee jerk epiphanies.
Left a note by the bureau,
 Its all in there.
Just to hard otherwise, all that jaw'in
Much easier to reach peace in silence.

I prepare for an over wearied age.
Through the gray.
Past the veiled lightning.
Treasured between
Life and death.
Down below the almond scent of pain
 Lies the gift of sight.
When all worries settle to the bottom,
 And the wealth of white matter releases its secrets of the soul.

I awoke in the river.
Fighting the tide with the great bear.
Till I could swim no more.
The bear gave me his back
 And headed for the land between the sky and smoke.
The bear bled and turned the water crimson.
The crows watched with fierce zealousness.
Their murder began to extend beyond my sight.
Into the darkness that I feared the most.

Daniel Raven

Glory lies in the deceptive.
The agendas of man will haunt him.
When the owl comes,
 We must be ready to give.

This harsh world,
 This common earth.
It speaks to me in tongues.
Weeping healing rain.
Giving to the dead and unborn.

There is no innocence.
Only multiplicity of guilt
 And the ghosts
                    That linger
Further into this oddity of animation.

As the trees bend in argument,
 The ravens referee in the fallen snow.
Reserving their tricks for man.

In the time of the solstice,
 Under the red moon.
You will find my bones beneath the earth.
Learning lessons from the great mother.

My past produces a thousands of images I can not erase.
Like grainy 8mm.
Simplifying my complicated misery.

At night my spirit struggles with the memory.
The dream.
The perpetual moan of the wolf.
Through the wintery smoke and shade,
 Near the valley where my people perished.
I descend once again into the water.
As the fountain sings shitsaa iiniya
 And gives birth to the eagle.
Awakening the sky,
                         Below the breath of heaven.

To often I let this heart instruct.
Guide.
Mentor my affection.
How anemic these eyes evaluate the past.
They blur and bludgeon,
 Tear the tangible from the abstract.
Then murder indiscriminately.
Like buckshot in the wind.

Daniel Raven

This iris haunts.
As my mind mumbles reverberations
 Of this soul.
Both cavernous and obtuse.
It hosts my deepest miseries.
Serving them tea in the dark.

In with the old breed.
This wolf must lie beneath
 The crows,
                In solace.

Daniel Raven

My dreams are a chasm.
A watery vale
                Of the deep.
Where hope drowns in silence,
 Behind a curtain of tears.

That night we drank a six
 And fucked in the dirt.
I could swear you were all that remained of this world.
Your daddy's problem,
 The itchy grass.
Didn't matter.
Your bare freckled ass in the moonlight just seemed to float.
Like its own planet.
Makes me dizzy now when I think of you.
Wonder why life's pinnacle ended when I's just seventeen.

These desperate oaths.
Hallowed rituals.
Rancid relics of the past.
As this eternal night endures it seethes with a quietness.
Solemn as a church.
Deadly as a sorrow.

In The Kingdom of The Crow

Feast or famine.
One more horrid then the other.
Cheat or starve,
 Where's your God now?
He's broken you.
Owned.
High in the heavens lies salvation.
Down in the dirt lies you.
A face,
        A will.
A dirty Pagan with blood on his hands.
Boot deep,
 Wading in the worlds hypocrisy.

Daniel Raven

Wild we were
 And woven as one.
Like mimic moons we shared this time like others do
                    Yet.
When you spoke my heart wept,
 And all the earth caught fire.
Till there was nothing else within my sight.
Just the wild we possessed.
Just the un-quenchable
          un-imaginable fever that only few could even hope to dare
 and even fewer could adopt as their own.

Her madness was a compass for cruel lust.
A polluted gale of calm,
 And sad musing.
A suffering so deep,
 God thought of her,
  Every time it rained.

Daniel Raven

All things must return to where they begin.
When this time comes.
We will all receive a warriors peace.

This burn,
 It quivers in my rib cage.
Dispersing my pride.
Feeding my fears.
It whispers to it's legions,
 Succumb to me,

Succumb to me,
 And rest upon this dreary sea.

We were symmetry.
Perceptible to those present,
 Yet recluse in nature.
A breathing rhythm.
A fragile gaiety
                Broken by the wind.

At night my spirit struggles with the memory.
The dream.
The perpetual moan of the wolf.
Through the wintery smoke and shade,
 Near the valley where my people perished.
I descend once again.

Daniel Raven

I dream of a pristine awakening.
A collaboration of the euphoric at the moment of acceptance.
Negating all time and space.
An infinitesimal, arbitrary, Norse soliloquy.
Kneaded beneath the earth with the roots,
 Awaiting flight to Valhalla.

To wake and feel reborn.
I've been
 To long
          Asleep,
My shadow
 Exiled
          Deep.
My heart
 Bloody,
          And torn.

The past is a docile shadow.
Only accommodating to ones acceptance of defeat.

I have spent this life the sages way.
Obdurate to any obstacle.
Knowing this life, is but a seed.
Fertile,
 But fragile in all respects,
  And easily influenced by all things,
Atmospheric and telluric.

Daniel Raven

My mind,
Filled with mockery
Quietly creates a whirlwind of wandering,
 And weaves within the crests of images long buried
But not forgotten.

Between the glimmer and the spark,
Lies the truth.

I've been in this box before.
Held hostage by its walls.
Lacerated and left to inebriated squalor
I will
Unhinge its presence.
Its metaphoric penitentiary.
I will abscond.
If only for a short reprieve.

Constrained by the confines of this skull,
 I walk a calloused turnpike.
Itinerant between this life
 And the moss.

This cerebral carnival continues.
Angst,
      Worry,
           Doubt and disbelief.
Its torsional vernacular invades my slumber.
Like razors in a jar.

You walk about in my shadows.
An unutterable curse.
Candle in hand,
 Coaxing my memories with fallacious nostalgia.

Daniel Raven

I've done nothing to save myself from this oblivion.
I've only fed the monster further
Craving raw red meat at the door.

This shattered soul
Is cursed to inscribe
An array of requiem
Upon the thickened walls of this heart.
Until its very end.

Vision seeks out what it wants,
Then turns a blind.
Sought through sacred circumstance,
Infrequent movement,
 And hedged opaque clarity.
Till the window fills with years of dust and grit and faded cracks.
Yet the center lies newborn smooth.

I am a madman.
Leading a nation of utterances
 Within
To the brink of sullen hypocrisy.
How can I tend to ancestry when I cannot even quell
The legions
            Inside this skin.

Thankless prompts,
Broken words.
All perils which I cling to in ignorance.
Feeding falsehoods to my heart,
All the while never having dreamt of a life
 Beyond my anguished passion of the past.

When this famine
 Lifts the skin from my skeleton,
And my prophecies have all fallen
 Under the annals of this heart and mind.
This soul will bloom in the presence of affection
 And release the unwanted myths within.

I've become an accomplice in my own existence.
Longing for the darkness.
Hiding from the truth of the world.
The fevered dream,
 A frozen spectator.
Watching innocents hold back a legion of horribles
 Inches from the fray,
                    As I lay,
Swollen.
          With new found hindsight.

I pray.
Near nightly,
 That I may touch the visions of her sleep,
 And pierce her realm of pain before my tremulous heart
 Becomes a blessed sacrament for the earth.

The Coming

Diners open.
Neon's on.
Depressives,
  Insomniacs,
Lonely hearts,
  Drunkards,
The desolate and destitute.
Were all here.
Waiting on the specials.
Pull up a seat,
 Take the corner.
Suns peering,
 Displaying dust like a living carousel.
Steaks tuff, eggs runny.
Tabs always on me.

Welcome to the diseased.
The dried and swollen.
The walking hidden façade of your former self.
An illusion, nothing more.
Oblivious.
Where those who think fate is purgatory and dreams are the end.

This path before me presents an aperture of hope.
A moment of pure solace in an otherwise darkness of thought.
I pray it gives me sight and guides me on beneath
  the blackened twilight.
Beyond the thorn rimmed undergrowth.
I hope it believes in me, as I believe in it,
  And finds the pleasant nature to show me its end.

Daniel Raven

These hopes have found words.
A new found strength of which my spirits lofty
 Converse keep hidden from my heart.
In order to heal my soul.

I lack the strength to fear this earth
 As others would have me do.
To label it so.
As if to tame its awe inspiring ferocity.
 And encapsulate its advantage in darkness.

Life's a series of wasted moments.
False truths,
 And witty banter.
We all gotta fill the hole somehow.
Question is,
You fill yours with a shovel,
 Or a spoon?

There's an advantage to being broken.
To live outside the cracks
 And witness all the saddest tales the heart could ever tell.
Beyond what one could believe.
Abstinent and accursed,
Fragmented and out right driven to find the truth of it.
We all tremble at the thought of giving our being to another.
We fight and seethe and seek like slaves
 As if to plague this very certain desire in life.
There is a fine line between love and hallucination.
Yet both are equally maddening.

With you its always so simple.
So raw.
Like the earth christened it so.
Like the tides ebbed in our favor.
Fates fickle in its conception
 but truth,
the way I see it,
in your eyes.
Just like a star.
Bright and constant,
 Unwavering and unbreakable.
Lost in awe and left adrift,
Trying to tread water in those eyes.
Sinking deeper and deeper into you.

They said I's a maniac to wed some virgin bride.
Temptin that heavenly ghost to lay them burdens of sin upon us.
Like a resolute a nature.
But I don't listen,
 What do they know.
We's the children of God.
Sent down to save our sons from the bonds of purgatory.
Those who ain't risen yet are left in the shade.
Well,
I ain't been set upon the earth to judge my foes.
Ain't no gulf of hell in this heart.
Beat if you must,
Vengeance,
 Tyranny.
Hell becomes panic,
 Begets dolor,
                And leads to eternal damnation of the soul.
Like wrecks in a tempestuous sea.

Daniel Raven

Out of the dark,
A stirring is met alone.
There is a cry in silence,
 And a pair of eyes joins the great song of creation.
Under the Alamikos moon.

The salt of this earth.
The real grit,
 Lies in the light of thought.
An idea.
An obsession.
An unfiltered and unrelenting dream.
The kind that invades your disciplined chaos,
 And rearranges your life for the better.

Ain't nobody promised tomorrow.
So you live.
You live long n deep.
All in,
      Always,
And when you wake,
And that tomorrow come again
     Smile.
You've won another day.

I lie in wait, a hunter.
Whose breath the universe exalts.
Giving,
      Bestowing benedictions to the moon.
Awaiting autumn leaves and dancing within to the fall of a thousand
 Thrones.
Like all the devils behind them.

Daniel Raven

The sky it seeks.
Melting the fragrant earth.
Deafening the trees in angst
 And reverence.
A remembering of the old way.
Before man was ashen.
When mother earth would free its fears,
 With rain.

My spoils,
Doggedly divided amongst this split soul
Now only heeds a deeper privation.
A limitless exhaustion.
Where thoughts revolt
 And violence helps to dissipate the screams.

Daniel Raven

Dusk again.
Another day of unshed tears
 And emotional refuge.
Liquor loosens my warmth,
 As my breath curls a globed smoke past my brow.
Above the shrunken ash,
 Where thoughts lie silent in this unlamented tomb.

Amid the passions of my people
 Is the calming spirit.
Together we foresee the happy age.
Where the winds are mild,
 And the darkness light.

The abyss of my history,
 The lines on my face.
Proud roads of poverty.
Cracks.
Holes.
No shoulder.
Gritty an un governed.
A palpable map of loss.
Where my thoughts go to grieve.

Skies in heat today.
Every time it opens its mouth it shows red.
Like what flesh is to the bone.
High rolling,
 Patiently passing its breath.
Gentle on the down side,
 Its presence slight, like a paper cut.
The sky reaches all.
Touch the day.
Open your mouth.
Pass through.

Daniel Raven

My people are the color of night.
They speak with the wind
 And lightning.
And when my white arrow dances in the darkness.
The great spirit rewards me with bounty.

The shades of this evening have wrapped around this heart so tightly,
I fear it may never feel the sun again.
Floating from one faint hope to the next.
Its aberrations far from helpless aide to form the foundation of a
 tempestuous affair with the dreary night before me.
Until it and I are irreplaceable with each other.
As plain and empty as glass and left to mourn oblivion,
    Together.

Daniel Raven

These dark crimson bricks.
If they could only admonish,
 Warn the weak of their intention.
Collecting essence through these narrow halls and streets.
Like hungry pot holes on the highway.
Since genesis it feeds.
As fluent as the river that runs beside it.
Always aware,
Always composed,
Always present upon your lips,
 In your drink,
                    Behind the object.
Born of words.
Nurtured by credence.
Molded into legend.

I grab it firmly from the shelf.
My nightly ritual.
A wet and calming oasis in my desert of confusion.
Two cubes and pour.
A Non-newtonian viscoelastic fluid,
  Yet just as vital for sustainment,
    Sanity.
I hide it, and it hides me.
Shuts me off from the rest of the world.
As I lie peacefully in its bosom.
If only for a couple of hours before the dawn.

Life is time.
Nothing more.
Don't waste it on the past.
Don't dwell on what could have been.
LIVE.
Live and love in the smallest of pleasures,
 With the greatest of hearts.

As faint and weak as a thought.
This bleeding logic shall become an end.
An enigma,
 An abyss that will swallow all of me and scatter like dust,
 Like strange property among the stars.

When last I looked my pelt was warm from liquor.
And I,
 Unvaccinated by suspicion,
Inexorable, and linear retraced my steps through the snow
 In search of forgone conclusions.

This snow will not last.
Before it dissolves
 And turns the sky a murky gray,
The timber wolves will bane beneath its splendor.
And have the final word of the night.

In the earth lay my family.
My people.
Once proud,
 Lucid,
  Humble.
I look on to them.
Embrace their memory.
For only they shall bless my future.

Above the curl of the new bent moon
One lost soul with woven flame.
Must cater to his ugly wounds
From a girl, a vision, that bears no name.

The sky it casts such sweetened sleep
Like the tides it ebbs and flows.
It harbors the secrets we often keep
And binds us from what we mustn't know.

This poor lost soul
This harbored flame
This solemn girl without a name,
This weary walk and full disdain

It can not end this way.

For if he fights and just resists
If he seeks instead of sews.
His heart and mind will still persist
And win this girl whose name he knows.

Daniel Raven

I will live for you.
Curl thick smoke
 So you might see.

   My promise to you.

Under this moon
This night,
We shall make the future.

Whether my fate is quietus with sin
  Or any other altered rebirth.
When the gates of darkness close
  This soul shall bend in shadow
    And repent upon the soft oblivion of all my fears.

Deaths dedicated groom.

I will fall to divines judgment willingly.
Knowing you saved me once,
  And so shall you again.

Dear sky,

Where do we end?
Is there still room between them stars?

I want to believe.

This hedonist heart haunts my state of grace,
I swear it.
Subtle as a tack hammer.
How long must I wait beneath the earth,
Till mercy come and grant me peace.

I knew good from evil.
Still I chose the latter
 And feasted on her skin of rage
Of fear
         Anxiety
               Revenge.
Her hallowed eyes heaven wide
 Held me hostage.
As her thighs held me hopeless
 With such caustic
         Steady rhythm .
Until she emptied all of me
 And left my heart to die.

The morning violets violate my vision.
Set upon a window in the sun.
They hold my hesitant heart hostage,
Blocking my straining view of what's to come.

A polluted current runs through these veins
 And toils
            On the spoils
Of love and war.

Daniel Raven

One day the night will close all around,
 And my soul shall sing

    Of unspeakable death.

Destined.
I will arise, only in your dreams.

Repent upon the irrevocable.
These weak wounds,
 Received in hospitality
Only honor the infamous
 Through vain idolatry,
        And evil in God.

Fight

Live you bastard live!
Pick your teeth up,
Throw that armor away

Wont need it.

Go on, lead wit your head.
 Lean in.
            Get close.
Two to the cage outta do.
Drag that prize home.
Bathe in its blood.
Smile you caw,
Victory.

Vivisect these sensorial wounds
And arise
      A better man.

If you gonna make a deal
 With the devil,
You best be light
 On your feet.

Cause whether or not
 You permit it,
That ole Devil he plays things
 To keep.

Daniel Raven

Bound for the dirt
Where legions live
 And evil incubates beneath the dry church grass.
The wind, their eternity.
A mirror,
        Be it joy or sorrow.

Treachery tricks the naïve
But salivates the evil.
Granting permission to pass
For a price far beyond its burden.

Nature preaches if you listen.
She conceives all difficulties
 And consoles.
The mighty arise across her brow.
Strong is the great mother.
Whether her heart lay on the left,
 Or the right side of man.
We need only to blush,
 And ask forgiveness.

Before the weeds surrounded our atheism.
Choke the dirt from our teeth.
You should know.
  It was freedom, pure and simple,
    And before the air left my lungs eternal,
I knew it so.

My fears fornicate in the dark.
They mix with liquor
 And the hazard of inestimable loss.
Loud they grow through expeditious parliament.
They feed the monster within.

I cannot see into the future,
 But I trust in it,
                    With all my heart.

She who tamed the nights watch over the sky
Has fallen under the stars weight for the last time.
Meeting her maker with gnashed teeth
 And challenging all,
  Animate and inanimate
   Under the changeling moon.
For with her demise comes
The barren
The fruitless
The decayed.

Give that man enough whiskey an he'd sing to the heavens bout the
devils plight an how we's all accomplices in the war on our souls.
   Blah D Blah,
   Christian squealing.
   Ain't no deavil beat me true.
   I'm my own Judas among the sheep.
   Night skies just another backdrop on an otherwise mundane existence.
   Down in the mud.
   Nobody sees,
   Not like me.
Most folk gotta go climb a mountain to look at what's right in front of'em.
Saggy assed congregations.
Ain't no rhythm to life
 Just is.
Angels sigh,
Devil grunts,
Go on pull on that bottle.
Down deep lay the lies mans held onto for centuries.
The kind that quake terror in your throat.
Salvation.
Damnation.
Good.
Evil.
Jesus is callin,
Hummin in your ear momma'd say.
Come to light that darkened soul.

Daniel Raven

This world will forever insensibly transform the few,
The weak,
The minions ready to live,
 Breathe, and think in accordance with a mantra.
Under rules which are no longer the practical order.
Those that think this way,
That provide for the provider with malice and broken intentions under the guise of Gods will
 Will only fail.
As a man.
As a messenger.
As a leader.
In the end the dirt will cover us all,
 But the guilt will spread throughout the ether.

Enamored by this Eden.
I am left earth up
 Under the moonlight
To vex these dreams of you.

We shared this time like others do
With walks and dreams and gestures true.
Till both of us departed
Quite the equal brokenhearted.

And though there was no one in fact to blame
We left each other just the same
Both of us so very vain
In our decision.

So why does my brain recall all this now
Does it think there's an answer to these broken vows
Like an insight or a pinnacle thought on this how
Or why this past is so?

Only the Gods can foresee what's in store
For two truly lost souls
With no loving core
Two barren cold corpses
That feed on what's gone
No matter the suitor who holds them at dawn
Try though they might to fit in they are scorn
 To never feel true love.

When I awoke
 Your lips were cold.
Shades of twilight lay on our sheets.
A veil of tears
 And translucent fears
Assaulted me as I weeped.
And as the bed grew dark and absent
 And this heart fell old
And weak.
I no longer knew of life
 and love
but only eternal sleep.

Daniel Raven

Take an act of God to move this maladaptive liver
Off its stool and into the sunlight.

Guess you'll leave me now that the myths made flesh.
Still.
 That touch seemed enlightend.
Reminiscent.
All cognizant of its intentions.
Its betrayed bodies before,
 And explored there ash after.
Your little lost legion made of skin and tears.
I absolve to its inevitable.
I atone,
 And admit.
Never did I want a more winsome death.
Then by the beauty of you.

This road ends soon.
Turn in your invincibility.
Fears,
 Passions,
   Anything human.
Provides the opportunity for self admiration.
A façade,
 The man who thinks.
Time to mash the petal.
Throw the last 10 into the wheel.
Grin you sumbitch.
You're free.
Taste the heat from the engine block.
Let it soak deep in the bone.
Feel that existential quandary,
 And don't you ever,
                        Look away.

While traveling down the river styx
I noticed it beyond the yucca trees.
Singular,
 And circular.
It bit the tree tops as I advanced towards the rivers edge,
Then bent down the valley casting a dull red shadow
 Across the bog.
Giving birth to the darkness.

Dare to dream immaculate.
Past insignificant martyrs.
Knee
Deep
 In the mire.
Its how its gotta be.
This life ain't pretty,
 These souls ain't soulless.
Preachers preach,
Bankers bitch.

 Words.

Pick your poison,
 Lay it out
Stark.
Like an instinct.
Find your peace and swig.
All them other deities can wait.

Its funny how fast liquor goes from celebratory,
To sin in the eyes of judgment.

Daniel Raven

The worlds a tattered coffee table,
Dressed up like a stage.
Give me innocence,
Give me farouche,
Give me unhinged existentialism,
Give me cerebral enlightenment.
Show me another face,
 And another.
Were all just a carousel of cautious children.
Still afraid of the dark.

My heart breathes more than my lungs could ever aspire to.

Daniel Raven

Cold is the light beneath these fallen shadows.
Weak are the peacekeepers of the faithful.
Warriors to the hordes of flesh.
They hold no sway onto this oblivion.
They serve only as false hindrance to the gilded cage.

You are my destiny.
I feel it.

I hate you.

The way you make me feel.
All weak in the knees like in them movies.

I see how you stare at the stitches on my dress.
Dirty'in up them blue eyes with sinful aspirations.
And I feed into them eyes,
  Adjust my walk so as to invite a little lift in my hem.

I can feel you.

    Watchin me.
Cursin the wind for not cooperating.

Talk so sweet you give a girl a cavity and I just eat it up.
Picturing the day you gonna come sweep me off my feet,
  Make a proper woman outta me.

You ain't though.

Daddy says its just a fever,
One of many,
Itl pass.

Still.

My chest burns s hot.
You'd think the coals of hell fire was commiserating with my loins.

Who knew destiny would cause so much pain.

Daniel Raven

It was the witching hour,
Where great deeds were no more alone
 Then the very presence of your wintery heart.
When the quietus that fell upon the room
 Seemed to often loom for what seemed like an eternity.
Where great thought and valiant effort seemed to render logic useless in
 The end.
Why must I wake every night at this peril, of this hour?
Have I not won the right through the slaying of daily demons to set
 My mind at rest from such mental treachery?
The walls seethe,
 Then bleed convalescence as I listen to what's left of this
 Hearts dreary worn out valves,
  And wonder how they still go on without you.

The sorrows of this world are so
  Strikingly vast
  Dismal
   And gray.
They make heavy the means of my travel.
Behind every shadow seems to lurk
  The pestilential vices of man.
Who am I to cry illusion.
Perhaps the hard truth is more than a mournful burden.
Perhaps it's a trip through this heart
  That is to blame.

Nomad.
No direction,
 No mercy.
An animal unleashed.
Present among my angst
 My body prepares for war,
So my soul can live in peace.

The world itself gleams with
The uncanny fore-taste of
 A bitter memory.
Then hides in a tabernacle of dirt.

James left his mind bout an hour ago.
Saw it in his eyes,
Right before the hole machine came outta his jeans

Then.

Holes a plenty.
On straight through the ice box size a my thumb,
 Milk stain'in poppas wood floor, makin it shine like the Regency.

Two in the floor.
One in the ceiling.
One through the window
 And two in the pantry.
You could feel the wind in their rage.
Whisperin hate and halting in objects.
Expressin their detest with song.

When darkness fell upon her eyelids
 A moments paradise in sleep.
The wild flowers embraced her fully
 Their roots so long and deep.
The morning vapors kissed her lips
 A gentle hiss, then sigh.
Its shape a summer melody
 Its wind a soft goodbye.

Winds waitin,
Plottin.
Planning to swoop down n steal my breath.
Sudden like a shot.
Pierce your chest n freeze your ventricles
    Hold'em there raw
Exposed.
Like they was on trail for abandonment.

This room.
These walls.
This perdition persists on pushing the very envelope of my patience.
They sit in silence and judge.
Eggshell stained,
 Off white ocular protagonists of scrutiny.

    DESIST!

Hold your hollow perspicacity somewhere else.
What do you know of the world?
Solid pillars,
 Nothing more.
You shall listen to my type, and speak, and rant.
Retain my tears,
 Absorb my blows.
Just as those before me.
Now watch me pour another you horrid gauge of habitation.

Praise be to Jameson.

Daniel Raven

Lester ain't capable of rhythm.
Poor fool.
Just leaps up and gyrates.
Like he's gone limp in all his limbs.
Someone said he was a preacher before the war.
Saving souls by divinity,
 Washin feet and such.
Sometimes,
 After supper in the galley,
 After all the medications givin out
He lay long in the tooth about the Battalion a blaze and all the Japs
 Hittin the trip wires, turnin night into day amidst the smoke and debris.
Beth and Agnes always say "Poppycock!" and turn in early.
They say ain't no man made abomination can turn the nights sky red,
Only God.
Still.
I wonder.
Sittin there, listening to Lester draw all the oxygen outta the room leaves
 me ,
      well,
Breathless.

Tomorrow I think I'll ask him to dance.

This raw life
Leads on in sickness.
Through jagged cobblestones.
Past dreams,
Past hope,
Past the last stop this train has to offer.
Draggin this lifeless sack a meat.
Relying on inertia

G
R
A
V
I
T
Y..

Praying for momentum.
Determined,
 Focused on solace.

Daniel Raven

Thelonious Clay was a large man.
Looming,
 Long winded patriarch.
Always preachin with his right hand on account of his left
 Got sliced off long ago.
"Lakota Devils!" he said.
Came in high from the ridge.
"Ambushin Cowards".

I suspect not.
Lakota don't lay in wait.
They don't disingenuously disgrace their ancestors by way of trickery.
Never saw a man lie with such grace.
Like the Devil himself gave him his tounge.

I'm an outlaw.
It's all I know.
Legit will always be a dream.
An impossible achievement.
I'm in so deep my nightmares hunt each other,
  Defining my character for the day.
Hard.
Evil.
Cold.
Ruthless.
Unmerciful.
The night forgives but I do not.
I cannot afford forgiveness.
I cannot afford to pray.
I cannot afford,
  Your love.
I'll leave this world the way I found it.
Then let the Devil be.

Daniel Raven

Bones haven't shaken like this in years.
Not since the summer of 52.
Can still smell the angry essence of her dead flesh.
Basting in the solar like some precious feast.
Momma said eternal evil lay latent that day.
Told her it was pointless to teach a child to read.
Ain't no Angel by way of gospel gonna come down an
 Save her from the weeds.
Ain't no wraith strong enough to chide mommas
 Wrathful temperament.
Sun just kept on cookin.
Stingin my eyes
 Draining my throat.
Took two weeks to settle in with the top soil.
Never did have tomatoes so red.

I was on the great bridge again.
The one that spans the journey between our souls,
 And leads to our one true nature.
It was cold,
                    Weightless.
Yet peaceful and inviting,
 And all the colors of the universe danced above my head.
A mingling menagerie of marvelous energy.
All the life before.
A collection of controlled animation.
There, on the bridge,
The Crow took flight,
 And pierced the endless atmosphere.
Reanimating my spirits creation.

In   the   end

we

are

born.

Made in the USA
Lexington, KY
08 November 2017